The most effective way to destroy people is to deny and obliterate their own understanding of their history.
*   – George Orwell*

This book is dedicated to those whose history was denied and obliterated for too long.

Justice, Justice you shall pursue.

-- Deuteronomy 16:20

Based on a true story.

Prologue:
An Unexpected Phone Call

It was springtime. Carol was about to go outside to cut some of her garden's roses. She loved the scent of roses – her father's favorite flower. She had been thinking a lot about her father Charles lately. She thought about him today. She missed him so much these last three years since he'd passed away. As she headed outside with her pruning scissors, her telephone rang.

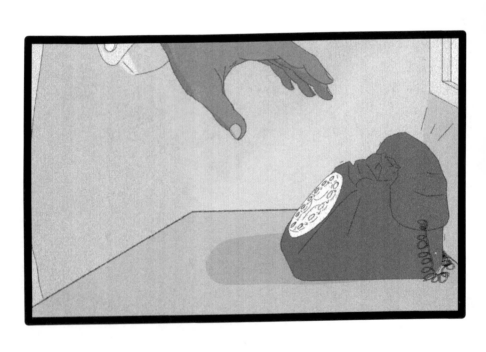

"Hello?" Carol answered.

"Hello, my name is Josh. Are you Ms. Greenlee? Ms. Carol Greenlee?" asked the young man on the other end of the phone.

Carol hesitated. Why did this man know her name and what did he want with her?

"I know about your father," he said. "I know justice wasn't served. And I want to help."

Hesitant, Carol listened as Josh told her:

"I'm a university student and, in class, I read about what happened back in 1949 in Groveland. I'm so very sorry for your family's suffering. Just now, I was driving back to school and passed the road sign for the town of Groveland and it hit me: I can help right this wrong."

Carol was interested but she had her doubts. Others had tried to help over the years but it always seemed to go nowhere. After Dad's passing, some family members encouraged her to move on. Maybe it was time to do just that, she'd thought to herself from time to time.

"I'm just a student but I have some ideas for how to help," Josh continued.

Still uncertain, Carol arranged to meet in person the next week.

Jim Crow Laws

The American South was severely damaged by the Civil War. Whole towns had been burned to the ground, ruined crops devastated the economy and it was next to impossible to control unrest. The US government tried to rebuild and reintegrate the South back into the Union. It established **Reconstruction** to keep the peace and ensure a smooth transition to a free society.

Former slave states resented these efforts and, to get around them, passed laws that limited freed slaves' choices by keeping them in debt and paying them meager wages in hard labor jobs. Freed blacks could not vote, could not be educated, and risked arrest for just about any reason. Their work and travel was restricted. They had no options under the state and local law. These laws effectively kept freed blacks enslaved.

For the next one hundred years, the South used these **Jim Crow laws** to segregate – or separate – black and white people in all aspects of life. Schools, restaurants, hotels, busses and all other public spaces separated black and whites. It was illegal for white and black people to marry one another. There were also laws designed to prevent blacks from voting. Jim Crow laws existed from the end of the Civil War until they were finally abolished in 1965.

Through Jim Crow laws, public spaces and privately-owned businesses segregated – or separated – black and white Americans in all aspects of daily life.

A Week Earlier

After a restful winter break, Josh kissed his parents and got in his car to head back to college. *This will be my best semester yet*, he thought.

A couple of hours into the ride, Josh entered Lake County, Florida, home of a large number of citrus groves, supplier of orange juice for breakfast tables all over America.

Josh looked around. Time seemed to stand still in this rural landscape. Lake County remained a bunch of dusty citrus towns and back roads in north central Florida.

And then he saw it. The road sign simply read "Groveland, Florida."

Thoughts instantly flooded Josh's mind.

I can't believe this is where it happened. How could four innocent youths be convicted of a terrible crime they didn't commit? A crime that never even happened? Where was the Law?

It was mind-boggling to Josh.

Josh recalled the facts he had learned in class: back in 1949, four black youths were falsely accused of kidnapping and attacking a white housewife. Despite overwhelming evidence that the boys were innocent, local police beat the youths into false confessions. Ku Klux Klansman demanded the boys' heads and burned down black homes and businesses for revenge. Before it was over, two of the youths were dead at the hands of the Klan and the Law, and the other two spent many years behind bars, a ruined past that was all too quickly forgotten.

The Ku Klux Klan

The **Ku Klux Klan** ("KKK") is a **white supremacy** organization in the US opposed to civil rights for Blacks, Jews, Catholics, gays and other ethnic, racial, social or religious groups. White supremacists are associated with acts of terrorism, mob violence, lynchings and other murders, and burning of homes and businesses.

Immediately after the Civil War, in the 1860s, Confederate veterans started the KKK to intimidate newly freed blacks. The KKK grew during the 1930s and 1940s Great Depression when poor whites who faced hard times blamed their financial troubles on blacks and Jews. This KKK was not just in former Southern slave states; it now grew across the country and had major political influence. Some politicians and law enforcement officers were members of the KKK.

Many whites, primarily in the South, disliked the KKK's violence but generally agreed with its view that white Christians were superior to other groups. After World War II, the KKK grew stronger in the South, where whites wanted to suppress black voter registration efforts and other legal victories for minorities.

Today, although much of society's views are generally more tolerant, white supremacist groups are still active across 41 states including Florida.

In the 1940s in Lake County Florida – many white men, including law enforcement, businessmen and local politicians -- were part of the Klan. Others who were not official members were in agreement with the Klan's views that the white race was superior, or "supreme."

Chapter 1:
Wrong Place, Wrong Time

Charles was a 16 year old country boy in July 1949. He left home that summer to look for work in the citrus groves of Lake County.

Just a few months before, tragedy struck when his 4-year old sister was killed on the train tracks near their home. Unimaginably, a few weeks later his 2-year old sister shared the identical fate on those very same tracks. His parents' grief was immeasurable and there were still eight children to feed. And Charles was soon going to be a father himself. He knew he needed to leave his tiny town near the Florida-Georgia line to go out and make it on his own.

Citrus picking season was starting up and Charles figured he could get a job in the groves, so he hitchhiked 100 miles in the hot Florida sun to find himself a job.

The Florida Citrus Industry

The first Spanish settlers brought orange seeds to St. Augustine in the 1500s. Today, most oranges and grapefruits sold in the US come from Florida. The orange juice on your breakfast table may very well have come from Lake County, Florida!

Central Florida is home to some of the nation's largest citrus groves. During the Great Depression, citrus became the leading business in Lake County. In the 1940s, the vast majority of people in Lake County worked in the citrus industry.

This big business was exclusively owned by whites who relied on cheap black labor to work the fields and packing plants. Owners tried to keep their workers' wages as low as possible to keep as much income for themselves. With many local boys off fighting the war, there weren't enough workers to meet demand. Local law enforcement worked closely with owners to see that anyone who could work did just that, for as little wages as possible, often seven days a week. Those blacks that didn't obey were arrested or beaten; those who tried to complain faced possible mob action and some eventually fled never to return.

Although most blacks worked in citrus, a few managed to acquire their own swampland and turn it into farmland. It angered local whites that these blacks worked their own farms rather than as citrus pickers or as maids in white homes.

In the city, Charles met up with Ernest, a young man he worked with earlier that year at the Humpty Dumpty Drive-In.

Ernest was older and had been around the big city. He suggested they head to Lake County where citrus jobs were plentiful for a tall, strong boy like Charles, even if the pay was poor. Ernest grew up in Lake County; his mother owned The Blue Flame, a juke joint on the outskirts of Groveland.

Juke joints were country shacks in the 1930s through 1950s found throughout the American South where black townsfolk could enjoy a few drinks, dance to live music and maybe even do some light gambling.

Ernest and Charles hitchhiked their way to Groveland on the back of old pickup trucks and arrived by late afternoon dirty and tired. Ernest's plan was for the two of them to stay at his parents' house as they looked for work. Charles decided to stop at the railroad depot to rest a bit while Ernest went home to get him a change of clean clothes. Charles never imagined that Ernest would never return.

African Americans in World War II

Black Americans have always played an **important part in US military history**, serving honorably since the American Revolution. Up through World War II, the military was still segregated; black soldiers could not fight alongside white troops.

World War II saw important African American inroads into fighting units. The first black pilots in American history were the famous Tuskegee Airmen who flew bombing raids in World War II. Towards the end of the War, black soldiers fought in previously all-white units in some of the fiercest battles ever fought in US history. Along with their white counterparts, black soldiers helped win the war. After the War, President Truman ended segregation in the US military.

African Americans were proud of their distinguished military service. Yet black veterans returned to an American South where prejudice against black people remained. To show their pride in their war service and their continued frustration with Jim Crow laws, black veterans would occasionally wear their military uniforms around town. Local police and white townspeople saw this as defiant and were hostile towards black veterans in uniform.

The Tuskegee Airmen, the first African American pilots in the US Army, were one of the most distinguished units to fight in World War II.

Chapter 2:
A Night on the Town

Walter and Sammy were young men just back from the war. They were proud of their military service overseas where they fought hard, sometimes side by side with white soldiers.

It was a tough adjustment returning home to racist Lake County, where blacks were reminded daily that their place was not side by side with whites.

After a hard week's work on Sammy's daddy's farm, Walter and Sammy were excited for a night on the town. Groveland was quiet and dusty, not much to offer young men looking for a night of "juking" – dancing and drinking and flirting with girls. So they headed an hour away to the big city, first Orlando, and then on to Eatonville where they knew the nightlife was more exciting.

An hour earlier, a young white couple had been driving through the dark night on their way back home from a country dance. Their car had been giving them trouble when it unexpectedly stalled amidst the orange groves.

Annoyed at their dilemma, and tired after a long night of drinking, the couple bickered by the side of the road. This was not the first time; in fact, they'd been living apart after a previous argument left the young woman bruised from her violent husband. She was back living at her parent's home; their marriage was on the rocks and her father had been encouraging her to end it while she was still young and without children. But she wanted to give it another try; this night had been a reunion of sorts, to see if they could work things out.

Their attempts to restart the car unsuccessful, they were stuck there for some time. This was not to be the reunion she hoped for.

After some time, headlights appeared. Sammy and Walter were driving down the same dirt road on their way home from their night on the town. Seeing the couple on the side of the road, Sammy and Walter stopped and offered their help.

The woman recognized Sammy; their fathers' farms were nearby one another. She knew Sammy and Walter were just back from serving in the war and were working on Sammy's family farm instead of the citrus groves like most other blacks in town. She knew all too well that her father thought Sammy's father was one of those "uppity" blacks because he owned his own farm rather than work for whites. And, her father complained, Sammy's brother was always showing off, driving his new car around town. The young woman recalled how her father cussed under his breath when he saw Sammy proudly wearing his army uniform around town. No question about it: her father – like most whites in town – didn't like black townsfolk who didn't know "their place."

The husband hopped behind the wheel to try to jump-start the car while Walter and Sammy pushed the car from behind. He barked orders at the two men. Despite their efforts, they could not get the car started. The battery was dead.

Seeing that the two men were pushing hard, the young housewife offered Sammy and Walter a drink from the whiskey bottle she and her husband had been passing back and forth between their lips all night. Hot and sweaty, the two men gratefully took sips right from the bottle and passed it back to her. But her husband – annoyed about the car and drunk from the night's activities – was now angry that she would dare to share their bottle with two black men; he exploded with insults at the two men who had been kind enough to stop to help the stranded couple.

Sammy had enough of this man barking orders and hurling insults so he grabbed the man by the shirt. With just one punch, the man – drunk and much smaller than Sammy – soon lay knocked out cold in a ditch.

Sammy and Walter didn't think much of it. They'd had their share of run-ins with white country boys. So they drove off, leaving the wife standing on the side of the ditch beside her scuffed-up husband. They each went back to their homes, went to bed and got up the next morning for work with little concern for the quarrel with the white man from the night before.

Chapter 3:
A Murky Morning

As the sun came up, an older couple sipped their freshly brewed coffee. They gazed out their kitchen window just in time to see a young woman mysteriously get out of a small dark car. It seemed strange, the couple would later recall, that the driver – a white man – would drop this woman off in this tiny town twenty miles from her home and quickly speed down the dirt road. They wondered aloud to each other why this little white woman would be hitching a ride out here on her own.

An hour later, a young coffee shop owner was up early to open his family's shop when he spotted this same woman walking by the side of the road. Like the older couple, he too thought it peculiar that this young housewife – unruffled in her pretty dress – would be out here alone so early in the morning.

He invited her in and they chatted awhile. Later he would tell police exactly what she told him: she and her husband had a dead car battery when some black men came to help. Trouble followed, she said. Foul words were exchanged and her husband was hit over the head, maybe left for dead. She claimed she left with the men in their car.

As he heard her account, the shop owner eyed the woman anxiously. He worried about a young white woman alone in a car at night with black men and asked if the men hurt her. She clearly said no, he later recalled to police. She seemed unconcerned about whether it was even appropriate for her to be alone with these men. He knew that in Lake County, only a white woman with a questionable reputation would find this situation unremarkable.

She offered no details about her time with the men and only grumbled of her aching feet. She did not seem particularly panicked for her husband either, he noted, which was peculiar because she just said her husband might be lying dead in a ditch. Instead, she calmly mentioned she was looking for her husband after getting separated the night before.

The shop owner drove her to look for her husband. When they found him – barely scraped or bruised – the young couple chatted quietly and the coffee shop owner went on his way.

At sunup as his wife was just getting out of a stranger's car, the young husband – sober now – was clear across the other side of Lake County.

After reviving and finding himself alone by the stalled-out car, he managed to finally get his car running. He'd spent the early pre-dawn hours frantically driving around looking for his wife. He wanted to get to her before she hitchhiked her way back home to her parents and told them of the night's events. It was just what her father needed to break their marriage up for good.

At a gas station, he found an attendant. He told the man that *four* black men had beat him unconscious and kidnapped his wife. Soon, he had the sheriff's office on the phone and was repeating the same story.

Just then, the coffee shop owner arrived with the wife and reunited the young couple. Later, he would recall that she didn't seem overly pleased to see her husband or even relieved to see that he had only a small cut on his forehead; after all, she had claimed just an hour before that her husband may have been left for dead.

Josh met with Carol the next week for coffee and questions.

"I don't understand how your father became mixed up in all of this," he said. "He was sleeping in the railroad station, right? The night watchman saw him. The local police knew he couldn't have been anywhere near that white couple in the middle of the night!"

"Yes," Carol sighed, "but the local police were above the law. And the worst of all was the Lake County sheriff."

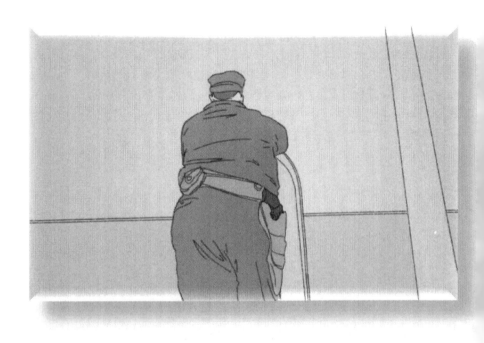

Chapter 4:
Above the Law

Lake County's sheriff was an intimidating man of the law. Known for his brutal reputation of violence and threats, he knew that a quick punch or whack with the butt of his revolver would keep the black folk "in their place." No doubt about it: he was the most powerful man in Lake County. His deputy and officers learned from the meanest man around.

Citrus grove owners relied on the sheriff to uphold the law and provide a steady flow of black laborers for the groves. In return, they re-elected him year after year.

With more work than available labor, the citrus grove owners needed more workers. They found their perfect man in the sheriff, one who strong-armed black people into working the groves – for low wages and often seven days a week. Those blacks seen "loafing" – taking a day off for church and family – were arrested for loitering and vagrancy; blacks quickly found themselves in prison where rough treatment by the police was the rule of the land.

The sheriff also had earned a tough reputation for squashing voter registration attempts through violence and intimidation. He hated the "uppity" blacks who tried to register to vote.

Black Voter Registration

After the Civil War and up through the 1960s, southern states made it next to impossible for blacks to vote. Potential voters needed to pass a demanding literacy test yet most African Americans received poor educations because of Jim Crow segregation and could not pass it.

States also required individuals to pay poll taxes to register to vote, which effectively prohibited poor people from registering. The literacy test and poll tax shut out poor and poorly educated blacks from registering. At the same time, the states shrewdly passed laws which allowed poor or poorly educated whites to get around these new literacy and tax laws.

People who were not registered were effectively shut out of the political and legal systems. They could not serve on juries nor hold political office. They also could not serve in law enforcement. In 1940, only 3% of eligible African Americans in the South were registered to vote. Almost all juries, politicians, judges and police officers were white.

In the 1940s, national black leaders knew they needed more Southern blacks voting in order to bring about change. They began **black voter registration drives** to help get as many blacks registered to vote as possible.

African Americans attempting to register to vote were met with state laws designed to stop them.

The sheriff grew furious when northerners came to town to talk with citrus workers about banding together to establish formal groups – or unions – for more rights on the job. It was his business to see that the only people with 'rights' were the grove owners – with rights to do whatever they pleased. He threatened and drove away union organizers who might upset the citrus business. He made it known all around Lake County how much he despised the "damn Yankees" who came from up North to try to meddle in his business.

The sheriff was out of town when his deputy sheriff got the young couple's early morning phone call. The deputy rushed out to meet the couple. After his questioning turned up many holes in their story, the deputy wondered if a kidnapping and attack on the young housewife had even taken place at all. It was clear to him that *something* had happened but he didn't know what.

The young couple's reputation around town wasn't great, the deputy knew. Everyone knew the rumors about the young woman from before she had married. Her husband's character was also questionable. His fights with his wife left her bruised and battered. He was a small guy with a ruddy complexion and didn't have a reputation as the brightest or the hardest working guy in Groveland. Surely police would laugh him off if they knew the truth – that he was drunk with a broke-down car when he got knocked out cold after just one punch. Instead, he thought, a story of four menacing men kidnapping and attacking his little wife would surely get some attention and ensure some action.

With four men now accused of attacking the white woman, the sheriff had the perfect excuse to clear Groveland of a few annoyances that had been bugging him. He'd get rid of four bothers in one shot, look like a hero to the citrus businessmen and set the black townspeople on notice that he was in charge. First, he'd show families like Sammy's and Walter's that Groveland didn't take kindly to blacks who thought too highly of themselves. He'd take them down a peg, he thought.

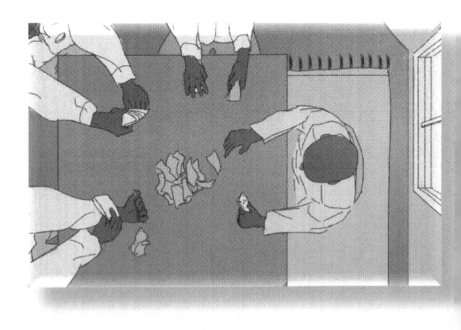

Next, he knew that young Ernest had been trying to break into local gambling operations, the second biggest industry in town after citrus. Ernest had been trying to cash in on the small time gambling in the back room of his mama's juke joint and the sheriff wanted to put a stop to that to gain favor with the other men in town who ran Groveland's gambling business. Connecting Ernest to this apparent attack would be a convenient way to put uppity folks like Sammy, Walter and now Ernest in their place, let them know who's boss.

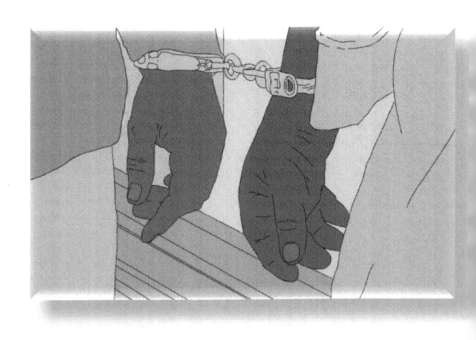

Sammy and Walter were getting ready for work early the next morning. They went about their usual routines, not giving much thought to the broken down car and the drunk and irritable couple from the night before. Soon, the police arrived to arrest them for kidnapping and attacking a white lady. Unworried, Sammy reassured his mother as the police took him away: "Don't worry Mama, I didn't do anything wrong. This will all sort itself out shortly." It must be a case of mistaken identify, he presumed, and he'd simply explain that to the police and be on his way, maybe even be on time for work.

By now the sheriff was back in town and not in a particularly 'sorting out' sort of mood; instead the police arrested the young men and immediately placed them in jail. The sheriff knew he had to get this situation under control before the weekend was over so everyone could get back to work in the groves as usual Monday morning. He knew there was a growing crowd outside the jailhouse windows demanding these boys' heads. He knew people were looking to him for answers.

The night before, young Charles had been taken by police to the local jail for loitering at the rail station but was assured he'd be released in the morning; unlucky for him, he was in the wrong place at the wrong time and that release never came. Instead – with the couple's story quickly spreading – the police needed to name a fourth man quickly before the situation got out of hand. How convenient for the sheriff that this poor boy from out of town had been in Groveland with Ernest the night before! With young Charles conveniently sitting in the local jail, this fourth young man was as good a choice as any.

Police Brutality & Lake County

Police brutality is the purposeful use of unnecessary violence carried out during law enforcement activities.

For centuries, American slavery included systematic and intentional violence against black people. After slavery, Reconstruction and then Jim Crow laws in the American South violently suppressed black people; police were often brutally unfair and racist in upholding these laws.

Lake County's sheriff was elected and served seven terms from 1944 to 1972. He shot two of the Groveland Boys while driving them to a new trial, killing one on the spot. Despite evidence that they were shot in close range while handcuffed together, the sheriff was not charged. He bragged that, In his 28 years as sheriff, he was investigated 49 times for police brutality and one time even stood trial for murder of a mentally challenged prisoner but was never convicted (by all white juries).

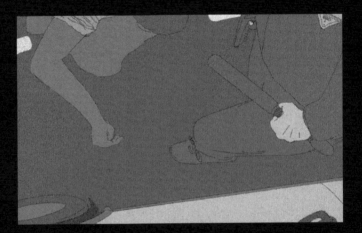

With three young men now in custody, the sheriff was ready to spring into action. Monday started a new week of work down at the citrus groves. He figured he'd wrap this up quickly in his usual manner.

All three men were taken one by one to the depths of the jailhouse cellar and severely beaten in a brutal attempt to force them to confess to a crime they didn't commit. Walter, the first to be taken, was beaten not once but twice, so badly that he was within an inch of his life and still refused to confess. The other two, seeing Walter thrown back into his cell half-dead, were sure they would be beaten to death and signed false confessions to avoid the same fate.

Chapter 5: Revenge

By mid morning, rumors of the alleged attack began to swirl around Lake County.

The sheriff was worried. He knew the Klan was angry. In Lake County, many whites were part of the Ku Klux Klan; they didn't need a legal trial to decide that black men accused of attacking a white woman were guilty.

Angry Klan mobs quickly gathered. They burned down homes and businesses in the black part of Groveland. Sammy's family farm was one of the first to go up in flames.

The sheriff knew that if he didn't stop the mobs from burning down the whole black part of Groveland, fleeing blacks would have no homes to which to return. He was all too familiar with other places where angry mobs destroyed black communities and caused entire black populations to flee; black residents simply never returned. For Groveland, he knew that no blacks would mean no grove workers. And no workers could spell the end of Groveland's citrus business and the end of his career. He couldn't let that happen.

He needed to get this situation under control; he knew he had to appease the Klan as quickly as possible without destroying Groveland's black workforce.

Black parents knew that when white people started to react to the rumors, it could be dangerous – deadly, even. They encouraged their sons to lay low until the rumors blew over, so most young black men fled the area. One of those who fled was Ernest.

The mob went after those who fled, looking for the four men rumored to be involved in the attack. Armed with rifles, revolvers, rope and ferocious dogs, hundreds of men quickly formed hunting groups and put up road blocks looking for Ernest.

Within days, the mob had grown to a thousand men, with Lake County's sheriff, his deputy and neighboring county law enforcement now leading efforts. They were determined to get Ernest, dead or alive. They tracked him down 200 miles away.

Ernest knew the back roads well and gave them a long hard chase. But when they finally pulled his lifeless body from the dirt, it was riddled with over 400 shots.

Klansmen and other angry whites weren't content to burn down homes and chase a fleeing man. Rumor was that four men had attacked a white lady, and they knew that the others were being held at the local jail. The Klan surrounded the jail and demanded that police give up the accused for them to punish the black men with a "good, old fashioned lynching."

By mid day, hundreds gathered in an angry mob ready to storm the local jail and avenge the young housewife's dignity without regard to the law. The sheriff knew all too well that the Klan had done it in neighboring counties: reduced local law enforcement officers to powerless weaklings when they lynched black suspects before law enforcement could follow what at least might appear to be proper procedures for a trial.

The sheriff knew he needed to control the unrest and appease the angry mob in order to stay in power. To do that, he had to show that he was boss. And he had to do it swiftly.

"And so," said Carol "The couple's story really just grew out of hand: from two guys to four, from one punch of a smart-mouthed drunk to the kidnapping and assault of a white woman."

"Listen," she continued, "in the Jim Crow South, if Sam and Walter really did what that white couple said, do you really think Sammy and Walter would have been calmly getting ready for work the next morning?"

"Yeah, good point," Josh noted. He remembered from class that the boys' lawyer, Thurgood Marshall, tried to argue this point at trial, but the jury had made up their minds before even walking into the courtroom. He recalled how it happened...

Thurgood Marshall and the NAACP

Thurgood Marshall was a successful lawyer who worked his way up to become the **first African American judge on the US Supreme Court**. He became interested in the law at an early age when he was forced to read the US Constitution after being punished by his second grade teacher. He became famous for winning the 1954 case "**Brown vs. the Board of Education.**" At the time, black and white students attended separate schools where black schools were poorly funded, had few resources, and were often in terrible condition as compared to the schools of white students. The US Supreme Court sided with Marshall and, ever since then, black students have been entitled to the same education in the same schools as all other students.

Throughout his career as a lawyer, Marshall argued 32 cases in front of the US Supreme Court and remarkably won 29 of these cases. He is widely considered one of the greatest legal minds the US has ever seen.

Five years before the Brown school case and more than two decades before being appointed to the US Supreme Court, Thurgood Marshall was the top lawyer for the **National Association for the Advancement of Colored People**, or the **NAACP**. The NAACP is the oldest civil rights organization in the US. It works for equal rights for minority groups and even today still fights against discrimination in schools, workplaces, housing and public places. In his role as the lead lawyer at the NAACP, Thurgood Marshall came to Lake County, Florida from Washington DC to defend the Groveland Four.

Thurgood Marshall, the first African American judge on the US Supreme Court.

Chapter 6:
Justice Undone

Walter, Sammy and Charles knew they were in over their heads. Caught up in the racism of Lake County, the boys didn't stand a chance in front of a Jim Crow judge and jury. Their families did the only thing they could: they contacted the National Association of Advancement for Colored People ("NAACP") for help.

The local Florida chapter of the NAACP contacted its Washington DC headquarters for legal support for the Groveland boys. Thurgood Marshall was a brilliant lawyer who came from Washington to head up the NAACP's legal team for the Groveland boys.

The day before the trial even started, the morning newspaper showed four electric chairs, like it was a unescapable fate that awaited these young men. It seemed like Lake County had forgotten that in the American justice system, those accused of a crime must be considered innocent until proven guilty in a court of law.

A speedy trial took place. Shockingly, the woman's lawyer withheld medical records that proved she had never even been attacked. The sheriff pressured the coffee shop owner to make sure that his story matched the couple's story. Witnesses who saw Walter and Sammy in Eatonville twenty miles away at the time of the alleged attack were never called to take the stand at the trial. Crime scene experts knew that the footprints the sheriff claimed were Sam and Walter's had been faked by police, so these experts were never called to the trial. Charles swore he didn't even know Walter and Sam and had never seen them before. Charles had been talking with the night watchman at the train station and later was actually in the hands of local police over at the nearby jail when the supposed attack occurred.

Despite all of this obvious wrongdoing, the three youths went to trial. None of the overwhelming evidence in support of the four young men seemed to matter. The case raised more questions than answers. All the police had for evidence was a white woman's word against these young black men; but in Lake County in 1949, this was all that mattered.

The all-white jury convicted Walter, Sammy and Charles in less than ninety minutes. The judge sentenced Walter and Sammy to die in the electric chair; Charles was spared the electric chair due to his young age and was sentenced to a hard labor camp for the rest of his life.

Thurgood Marshall went back to Washington distraught over the trial's outcome but he was not about to give up. The case of police violence and phony evidence was so clear that he appealed to the US Supreme Court to reconsider the case for retrial. He knew a second trial in racist Lake County would never find the young men innocent to allow them to walk free, but he was hoping to try to save their lives. So he focused his efforts on overturning the rulings for Walter and Sammy . Maybe, he reasoned, he could get their sentences reduced from the electric chair to life in prison instead.

After hearing Marshall's argument, the federal court reversed the boys' death sentences and set a date for a second trial.

The sheriff was fuming. Who did this Marshall think he was, meddling in local Lake County affairs? On the night before the second trial, the sheriff was driving Sammy and Walter from the state prison where they'd been housed to take them to the local Lake County jail for the next day's trial when he claimed his patrol car had a flat tire. The sheriff pulled down a dark county road and got out of the car to check his tire. He later stated that Sammy asked to go urinate and that, when he let the two prisoners out of the car, they − handcuffed together − attacked him. He grabbed his gun and shot each prisoner three times. Walter survived by playing dead, but Sammy was killed instantly.

Walter survived three bullets. After he recovered, he told a very different story than the sheriff. He revealed that there was no attempt to attack the sheriff, that the sheriff made them get out of the car and shot them twice in close range. Apparently, the sheriff's deputy arrived shortly after and, upon seeing Walter still breathing, the deputy shot him again to leave him for dead.

Walter would have died had the sheriff not phoned in to reporters to cover the story; reporters showed up just in time to see that Walter was still breathing and got him to the hospital. FBI crime scene investigation later supported Walter's story and disproved the sheriff's claims.

An Unjust Justice System?

Throughout the 1940s, Thurgood Marshall worked hard to defend many poor African Americans caught in a racially unjust legal system. At the time, there were virtually no black judges nor jurors. Very few lawyers were willing to give these people good legal representation. Marshall went south to defend many of these cases.

After the first Groveland trial resulted in guilty verdicts, Marshall returned to Washington and successfully got the US Supreme Court to agree to a new trial because of a gross misconduct of justice during the first trial. He represented the Groveland boys in the retrial. He noticed that the judge and lawyer for the other side were good friends with everyone on the all-white jury, and he knew they would never find the Boys innocent despite there being no hard evidence of the crime. Instead, he hoped that by defending the Boys, he would help save their lives, reducing their sentences from the death penalty to life in prison.

Civil Rights leaders like Thurgood Marshall fought within the legal system to get unfair laws thrown out. Over the last 70 years, many victories have been hard won in the criminal justice system and in education, housing and employment laws to ensure greater justice not only for black Americans but also for any minority groups experiencing legal injustice.

Carol and Josh had been talking for what seemed like hours. "So, what happened to your dad and Walter?" Josh asked.

Chapter 7:
An Ending Never Ends

Walter recovered from the shooting and was getting ready for a second trial when the state's lawyer offered him a deal: skip a second trial – and its risk of another death penalty outcome – by admitting to kidnapping and assaulting the white woman. If he confessed, he'd avoid a trial and be given a life sentence in prison instead. Walter refused, saying he would not lie.

So Walter stood trial a second time with Thurgood Marshall as his lawyer. Once again, another jury of the sheriff's white friends found him guilty. Walter was sentenced to death once more. He spent three years on 'death row' where every day he thought it might be his last. After that, a new, more willing governor reviewed the case at the request of the NAACP and reduced Walter's punishment from the death penalty to life in prison.

And then one odd day after eighteen years in prison, the prison guard opened the jailhouse door and declared Walter free as long as he never returned to Lake County.

With the clothes on his back and not a penny in his pocket, at age 41, Walter walked out of prison in Lake County. His health was not good after the violent police beatings and the many years of hard prison labor. He made his way south to his sister Henrietta down in Miami. After almost half his life in jail for a crime he did not commit, Walter began life anew, this time working in construction.

A little over a year later, Walter applied for and received permission from his Lake County parole officer to return to Groveland to attend his uncle's funeral. His first trip back to Lake County would mysteriously be his last: relatives found him lifeless in his car on the side of the road just hours after arriving in the county. The sheriff's department, responsible not only for granting permission for Walter to return but also for reporting on mysterious deaths, declared that Walter had died of 'natural causes.' Some questions remained.

"And your dad?" Josh asked Carol.

"Well," Carol said, "he spent eight long years working hard labor at the state prison."

"Four months into this time, I was born." Carol looked up, wistful. "I missed getting to know my father when I was a little girl. He sure did love me though; he'd save up his meager prison earnings to buy me a small birthday present each year. It always meant the world to me to get one of those brown paper sacks with Daddy's gift!"

"My mother would take me for visits once a year," Carol continued, as sadness swept across her face, "until it became too painful for Daddy. He asked mama not to bring me anymore. I understand why he did that, it was devastating for all of us."

Charles worked hard in the prison system for eight long years. He was a very reliable prisoner, first working grueling hours on a chain gang and later doing construction work on the Florida highways. More than eleven years since that night when young Charles was caught in the wrong place at the wrong time, he was freed from prison.

Aged 27, Charles left Lake County for Tennessee where he married and started a successful heating and cooling business. He and his wife raised a family on the outskirts of Nashville until he died at the age of 78.

Chapter 8:
Re-Righting the Wrongs of History

Josh had been listening to Carol so intently he almost forgot why he had reached out to her in the first place.

"I think I can help," he said. "After reading about this case, I thought about making a film about this story, but then I decided I could put my skills to better use. With your permission, Carol, I'd like to start an online petition encouraging the Governor to exonerate The Groveland Four."

"We tried to clear their names a few years back, and even included the medical evidence that wasn't permitted in the two trials," Carol recalled. "But all of our efforts seemed to lead nowhere."

What is Exoneration?

Exoneration is a legal term that occurs when a person who has been convicted of a crime is officially cleared, usually based on new evidence of innocence.

It is not a Pardon where the convicted person is later found to be innocent of a crime that happened. Exoneration is legal recognition that the crime **never even took place**. The Groveland Four boys were not just innocent of the crime for which they were charged; the "crime" itself never actually happened. Medical exams concluded that the woman had never been assaulted as she claimed.

Walter Irvin, Charles Greenlee, Samuel Shepherd and Ernest Thomas have all passed away now. Still, this exoneration is important to clear their names legally to help their families and the Groveland community heal. It's never too late to right the wrongs of history.

"I had just begun to lose hope," Carol hesitated. "But I don't know, I just get the feeling that God sent you to me out of the blue for a reason."

"Let's do it!" she exclaimed.

"But before we do, I have to ask you, Josh, why are you fighting this fight?"

He looked straight at Carol and without hesitation said, "It's just the right thing to do."

Carol laughed. "Josh, at first I was hesitant because you can't trust a whole lot of folks over the phone, but I could hear the sincerity in your voice. So, yeah, let's go ahead and do this, I need all the help I can get."

Carol turned and looked at Josh once more.

"You know, Josh, I used to ask my father about pursuing justice but he always told me to put the past behind us and move on. Could you believe it, he didn't want to dig up the past out of concern for that woman?"

"He was never bitter. He would say to me 'Carol, understand this person has to carry this for the rest of her life.'"

Epilogue:
It's Never Too Late to Pursue Justice

Josh decided he wanted to make a difference and, in the fall of 2015, he launched an online petition seeking signatures to send to the Governor asking him to consider exoneration.

He and Carol became close friends, speaking weekly by phone. They reached out to other family members of the Groveland men, prompting their support as well.

A media campaign led to articles in newspapers all over the US. Pretty soon over 8,500 people had signed the petition. People from all over the US and even across the world have heard about this story and determined that it's never too late to pursue justice for those who can't speak for themselves.

Carol said she will continue fighting for justice.

"I hope if nothing else more people will know the truth because that's what matters: the truth," she said. "It's important for my nieces and nephews and brothers who came behind me to have this cloud above their heads taken away. They should be able to talk about their family and my father proudly."

In February 2016, Josh prompted his university's law school to host a formal discussion on The Groveland Four. The school invited surviving relatives of the four men and Gilbert King, Pulitzer Prize-winning author of *Devil in the Grove: Thurgood Marshall, the Groveland Boys, and the Dawn of a New America*.

After five years of researching his book, Gilbert finally got the chance to meet face to face with the relatives of Walter, Sammy and Charles. They came from near and far, united in their shared desire for justice.

The lecture room was packed with law students, relatives of the men, and the media. It was open to the public and members of the community were in attendance. Gilbert King gave a presentation and family members of the men spoke with bittersweet tears as they remembered their Boys. Then it was time for audience reaction.

One man stood up and said "I grew up in a house filled with hate. I grew up around racists. I grew up in Lake County. I am the nephew of the sheriff, he was the Devil in the Grove."

The crowd gasped.

"I cannot change the horrible events of 1949 or the injustices visited upon your families ever since." He choked back his tears. "All I can say is – on behalf of my family – I am deeply sorry to Walter, Charles, Sam and Ernest, and their families."

Carol stood up. With the wisdom of many years gone by, a smile spread across her face. "The past is never just the past," she said as she warmly hugged the man. "And it's never too late to hear 'I'm sorry.'"

The End.

Sometimes you have to look back at the past to figure out what's going on in the future.

— Josh Venkataraman

At the University of Florida Law School, February 2016.
Left to Right: Josh Venkataraman and his parents Vasan and Barbara; family of Charles Greenlee including daughter Carol, brother Wade, and son Tommy; front center co-author Ben Polsky.

You're Never Too Young to Help: Here's How

Spread the Word about Josh's petition and encourage your family and friends to sign it:

https://www.change.org/p/exonerate-the-groveland-four

Write a letter to Governor Scott asking to consider exoneration:

Office of Governor Rick Scott

State of Florida

The Capitol

400 S. Monroe Street

Tallahassee, FL 32399-0001

One person can make a difference, and everyone should try.
    -- John F. Kennedy

February 25, 2016

Office of Governor Rick Scott
State of Florida
The Capitol
400 S. Monroe St.
Tallahassee, FL. 32399-0001

Dear Governor Scott,

My name is Ben Polsky, and I am 9 years old and I live in Cooper City, FL. I recently learned about a historical injustice regarding the Groveland Four. I had the honor to hear the award winning author Gilbert King talk about the case of these 4 innocent boys convicted of a horrible crime they did not commit!

I listened with shock to the family members talk about their father and brother and the devastation the injustice caused their families. I am so moved by this story that I am writing a children's book about it.

I'm writing you today to ask you to consider exonerating these 4 boys. Over 8,500 people signed a petition agreeing with us.

I hope you will consider righting this historic wrong.

    Thanks for your time.

        Signed,
        Ben Morrison Polsky

Letter to Governor Scott by co-author Ben Polsky, age 9.   105

The arc of the moral universe is long, but it bends towards justice.
-- Martin Luther King Jr.

What started as a fourth grade school assignment morphed into something much more relevant and important to today's news. It seems like all too regularly, month after month, we sit together as parent and child and struggle to make sense of lives cut too short: Trayvon Martin, killed 50 miles from Groveland; Tamir Rice, just 2 years older than this young author; Eric Garner; Freddie Gray; Michael Brown and others. Even at the time of this very writing, we sadly add Alton Sterling and Philando Castile to the long list of victims of a criminal justice system rife with racial bias.

The pain is deeply rooted and the divide is real. And yet, we are hopeful. Today social media and cell phone cameras help expose fundamental rifts in American policing and race relations. And with greater awareness, we are called to action.

While adults struggle with racism, homophobia, religious hatred, anti-immigrant intolerance and other forms of bigotry, young people across this country are more accepting, more connected and more united than ever before.

We are hopeful that today's political and cultural wars mark the darkest moments before the dawn, and we will look back on 2016 as a turning point in our nation's consciousness, as young people lead us towards a brighter, more just tomorrow.

-- Nancy and Ben Polsky

August 2016

Acknowledgements

Deep gratitude to:

Josh Venkataraman

Barbara and Vasan Venkataraman

Gilbert King

Carol and Tommy Greenlee

Vivian Shepherd

Henrietta Irvin

Jake Rochford

This project is deeply informed by Gilbert King's page-turner and we are very grateful for his deep knowledge and his brilliant work of literature that made this historic episode come alive for us today. We were so fortunate to have spent time with Mr. King as well as the Greenlees, the Irvins and the Shepherd families and to hear their first-hand experiences. The Venkataramans welcomed our interest and efforts from the first interview all the way through to final editing. Thank you to Jake Rochford, an extended member of the Venkataraman family, for illustrating this book.

The warmth and supportive reception of a young boy trying to make a difference will be long cherished by these authors.

Bibliography

- Cosair, Gary. *The Groveland Four: The Sad Saga of a Legal Lynching.* Bloomington, IN, AuthorHouse, 2004.

- Hayes, Christal. "Groveland Four Families Thankful for Lake Apology, Still Seek Exoneration" *Orlando Sentinel.* March 15, 2016. URL: http://www.orlandosentinel.com/news/lake/os-groveland-four-families-lake-county-20160315-story.html. Last accessed: July 2, 2016.

- Hose, Aaron. *The Groveland Four.* 2003. URL: https://vimeo.com/7050259. Last accessed: July 2, 2016.

- King, Gilbert. *Devil in the Grove: Thurgood Marshall, the Groveland Boys, and the Dawn of a New America.* New York, Harper Perennial, 2013.

- Liston, Barbara. "Families Seek Exoneration in Florida Rape After 63 Years" *Chicago Tribune.* September 07, 2012. URL: http://articles.chicagotribune.com/2012-09-07/news/sns-rt-us-florida-race-rapebre8861er-20120907_1_groveland-four-groveland-four-charles-greenlee. Last accessed: July 2, 2016.

- Pitts, Jr., Leonard. "'Groveland,' An Injustice That Has Never Been Corrected" *Miami Herald.* September 26, 2015. URL: http://www.miamiherald.com/opinion/opn-columns-blogs/leonard-pitts-jr/article36702204.html. Last accessed: July 2, 2016.

- Stanford, Livi. "Lake Calls for Groveland Four to be Exonerated" *Daily Commercial.* March 15, 2016. URL: http://www.dailycommercial.com/news/article_3307490d-eb70-5405-a945-e619ff3e810a.html. Last accessed: July 2, 2016.

- Stone, Michael. "Behind the Search for an Apology in the Infamous 1949 'Groveland Boys' Case" *Time.* May 23, 2016. URL: http://time.com/4343491/groveland-boys-gilbert-king/. Last accessed: July 2, 2016.

- "The Legacy of Harry T. Moore" URL: http://www.pbs.org/harrymoore/terror/groveland.html. Last accessed: July 2, 2016.

- Vassolo Martin. "UF Student Fights for Justice for Accused Rapists" *The Independent Florida Alligator.* October 9, 2015. URL: http://www.alligator.org/news/campus/article_2e1ec960-6e43-11e5-b803-870d7f706aa1.html. Last accessed: July 2, 2016.

- Venkataraman, Josh. "Exonerate the Groveland Four" URL: https://www.change.org/p/exonerate-the-groveland-four. Last accessed: July 2, 2016.

Made in the USA
Lexington, KY
13 April 2017